Honeyfish

Lauren K. Alleyne

New Issues Poetry & Prose

A Green Rose Book

New Issues Poetry & Prose
The College of Arts and Sciences
Western Michigan University
Kalamazoo, Michigan 49008

First Edition, 2019.

ISBN: 978-1-936970-59-9 (paperbound)

Library of Congress Cataloging-in-Publication Data:
Alleyne, Lauren K.
Honeyfish/Lauren K. Alleyne
Library of Congress Control Number: 2018947283

Editor:	William Olsen
Managing Editor:	Kimberly Kolbe
Layout Editor:	Danielle Isaiah
Assistant Editors:	Andrew Collard, Alyssa Jewell,
	Sara Lupita Olivares
Art Direction:	Nicholas Kuder
Design:	Meghan Ganson
Production:	Paul Sizer
	The Design Center, Frostic School of Art
	College of Fine Arts
	Western Michigan University
Printing:	McNaughton & Gunn, Inc.

Honeyfish

Lauren K. Alleyne

New Issues

WESTERN MICHIGAN UNIVERSITY

Also by Lauren K. Alleyne

Difficult Fruit

I lie
dismantled. I feel
the hours. Do they veer
to dusk? Or dawn?
Will I rise and go out into an American city?
Or walk down to the wilderness sea?

—Li-Young Lee, from "Furious Versions"

This book is dedicated to my family—by blood and by bond. Your love continues to carry me.

Contents

III.

I.

Poetry Workshop after the Verdict

For Trayvon

Morning lights your four windows,
and you wake. It is, already, another day.
You stumble, befuddled, into the bathroom,
so white it's like you're inside the moon.
You look in the mirror, then turn away;
better to just leave. Get your body out the door
and into the blue day. You follow the brown—
sparrow, maybe?—perched outside on the rail
like a guide. Bring everything already packed
inside your skin—a dead brown boy and his free killer,
his judge and jury of women, the six *not guilty* bells
clanging again and again in your weary ear.
No, that's your alarm; it's time to be a poet.
You bring your pen and notebook, your poet's eye.
You try to follow instructions: *Write what you see.*
It's simple. You walk down the road,
safe in your pack of poets—women, white.
(You do not write this in your notebook.)
Instead, your eyes find and follow the lines
that run everywhere—across the street,
up the railings, across windows and shutters,
siding, shingled rooftops—parsing the landscape
into cells. Your white journal pages, ruled.
You write down all the signs: *Closed;*
Peter's Property Management; Not for public use;
These dunes aren't made for walking; stop.
But you cannot stop. You follow the wind,
ripe with salt and already-sweaty bodies.
You see a pile of beached boats lumped
like bodies in a mass grave; a stone wall drowning
while sleepy dories drift by; sun-bleached
stumps, slowly going to rot; You see
the sun marking time as it slips higher

and higher, the day stretching overhead,
last night's dark already memory. You see
an American flag, and below it, the reddening back
of a white boy lying face down on the sand,
his body the opposite of a chalk outline. You write:
the light skitters brilliantly atop the bay's piercing
blue. You write: *A boy, his light hair lightening to gold,*
his body, so still, still breathing. You write: *Not guilty,*
Not guilty, Not guilty, Not guilty, Not guilty, Not guilty.

How to Watch Your Son Die

For Miss Linda

When grief takes hold,
you monster through it.
　　　　　—"Oedipus," Rachel McKibbens

Watch his skin become a coffin
for his breath. Watch

his bones rise like phantoms
to haunt the twilight of his flesh.

Beneath the bedsheets of his lids,
see his eyes twitch, blind

and wandering; if opened,
they are the most beautiful glass.

He will unremember time
and laughter. His name

will become a strange music
in the foreign instrument of your voice.

Watch him lose each human border—
his tongue forsaking language,

his hands growing indifferent
to reach or touch, his heart sputtering

its final messages to yours.
Watch as he breaks from himself

and becomes a body so quietly
your tears thunder against his cheek.

Killed Boy, Beautiful World

For Aaron Campbell

How slender the tether
between life and not-life,
between the big-eyed boy
of your childhood play,
and the call that tells you
he is lying beneath a sheet
waiting to become ash.
How ruthless with beauty
the world seems, clouds
tumbling in streams of white,
the sky dappled, then clear,
then blotted with rain; the news
of death and more death
streaming—some familiar
or foreign blood damning
every wet curve of the globe.
Still, you want to hold on to it,
this life that breaks you again
and again. You want to know
that poised as the world is
to drive you to your knees
with anguish or ecstasy,
you are in it to stay
as long as it will have you—
as long as you have anything left
to lose.

Trojan Sun

It's fall on a winter day
and my island heart beams
like a sunflower
awash in welcome light.
But the dizzied roses
of my small garden,
caught between wither and bloom
remind me: November
thunder and short skirt winters
mean our planet is off kilter;
that a mild day in Iowa
shows up oceans away
as epic, unnatural disaster—
entire villages razed to splinters
by wind and water—the shifts
in weather around our globe
sometimes slow as evolution,
sometimes more big bang
for our brazen disregard
than we'd bargained for.
Already, it's too late for so much—
the ozone layer, disappeared
rainforests and ecosystems,
our dying oceans, the thousand
species gone extinct on our watch.
But here, it's a November morning
and from a clear sky, the sun
halos the bare trees with light
bright as fool's gold. Tomorrow
winter returns, dark and dank
in tow. For now, the beauty
of it all fills my heart to breaking
as I head out into our numbered days.

Post-Verdict Renga

For Trayvon

Provincetown, MA

Heat. Bodies gleaming with sweat and sun. Day pressing itself against everything: unforgiving. I am walking down this street thinking of another walk in another city, of a boy who never makes it home. I, too, am armed with thirst and a craving for sweetness; I, too, wear his brown skin and do not belong here, to this city of leisure and narrow streets. Fear passes through me, a phantom, and is gone. Overhead, flags flutter in the thick, salty air. *Not guilty,* they say. *Not guilty. Not guilty. Not guilty. Not guilty. Not guilty.*

Beginning is red—
a door, a car, the bowed lips,
a nameless flower.
*

I have so few names for things
here, I fall into silence.

Two men, black as God,
their shirts golden as morning.
No words between us.
*

So much passes in the glance
that the throat cannot muster.

Three headless torsos
in a store window. A light
trick makes men of them.
*

In this city of flesh, you
can almost forget the ghosts.

Fat daylilies crown
long green stalks, their orange heads
the color of grief.

*

No candlelight vigils here:
only the living, living.

He walks, oak brown, bald,
belly like a commandment—
I am here: make way

*

Nothing I say will save you,
but how can I say nothing?

Thick black curls cut close,
buttoned black shirt. Caramel face
diamonded with sweat.

*

a dark, ageless face
wise and innocent as earth—
how have you survived?

I can't stop counting
the bodies that look like yours:
five this whole morning.

*

I can't say if this matters,
just that I saw, I did see.

Play

An Elegy for Tamir Rice

I watched the video
        and wished I hadn't
and knew I had to

witness the boy
        being a boy before
he becomes a corpse

and the moments
        —brief as breath—
between his playing

killer and dying,
        between his shooting
the air and collapsing

(is that the word for it,
        the startled descent
of a child's bulleted body?).

I want to say *wait*
        but in the distance
between the urge

and the utterance
        between lung and lip
(one-a-thousand; two-a-thousand)

he is gone. I play
        the video again and again
trying to hit stop

in time to keep him
        alive. I make a black boy
Lazarus of him, minus

the miracle: the bullet,
        faster than fingers or hope,
wins every time.

The Pain Fair

The opening act is breaking
all manner of things open:
wishes, bones, hearts, glass
eyes, brains. They thud, splat,
smush and clatter into breath-
taking bouquets of new sparks.
A falling star actually lands,
hits the stage, becomes dirt.
We applaud politely: we know
this is nothing impressive.
The magician, slim as nails
waves his bony fingers
and everyone remembers—
first heartaches, first betrayals,
they resound like phantom
symphonies, notes swelling
our chests like air into balloons.
We gasp, full and fumbling;
the magician flicks his wrists
and the songs stop abruptly.
We make thunder. He bows.
For his last trick, he chants
in the language of the dead
and the ghosts come howling
their grief. Mothers and fathers,
siblings, childhood friends,
half-formed and unbreathéd
children charging like gusts
of humid wind. We breathe
them in and they pierce us
like so many shards; we melt.
The wails pour from us
wracked, wretched, we empty
ourselves like volcanoes,
hot tears scorching new roads
on our faces. He sings and sings,
our summoner, his voice rising
higher and higher until he, too

is wailing. For a long time,
we keen as one: the left-living
and the dead. The magician
strikes a gong, and the ghost-
winds leave us with little lingering.
We stagger to our feet,
exhausted, exhilarated,
our very selves shattered
and shimmering inside our bodies.
We stomp and hoot and whistle,
and slap our palms together,
feeling alive, that beautiful sting.

Still Life with Empty Beach

There is so much emptiness here:
the two chairs marooned on an empty deck,
the foot of space like a chasm between them;

the respectful distance the thatch of wild
grass keeps from their bodiless frames;
the frames themselves made of taut planks—

each holding itself apart from its neighbor;
each plank made of a million separate splinters,
some splintered from themselves. And deeper,

molecules, atoms, electrons circling nuclei
they never bump into. Everything moving
closer, closing in, but never completely.

What I'm saying is we are made of spaces
no thing can breach, bridge or heal—
not longing, not touch, not even love.

Self-Portrait with Impending War

Home is the hodgepodge house,
the vacant lot beside it, the ailing
mango tree, the stingy coconut trees
with nobody left to climb them anyway.
Perhaps, you think, home could be this
continent with its confused seasons,
the roads that roll out in front of you,
limitless as the night sky. Home be this
small silence you curl into anywhere you go,
the one hovering in your chest beating
its fleshy time. This planet you scar
with too many clothes and plastic bags: home.
And where to run but everywhere?
What to weep for, but what is going,
somehow, to be gone?

Untitled

For Anton

i. Graveside

The dirt has made way for you,
has heaved itself into a brown mound
beside the gaping hole in the earth.

The coffin arrives—a strange tree
we plant, wreath with rose blossoms,
water with tears. It blooms your name

in stone.

ii. Return

The cemetery is an untended field
I trample in search of your plot,
heels sinking into mud, the fear

of walking on the dead clamming
my brow with sweat. I tell myself
I would know your resting place

even without its marble address,
but I'm fumbling, and then give up,
despairing. You're not here,

anyway, I tell myself. Weep.

iii. Dream

If you could see me then/now,
you would tell me not to dissolve
like this, lose the thread of myself

in grief. I can almost hear you
urging me, *Doh take it so hard*,
if I strain, can summon your hand

on my shoulder, its weight.
But I know it's the magic of will—
me, trying to keep you real,

keep the living memories
unburied, your name's shape
on my tongue—all I have left of you

I cannot bear to lose.

Elegy for a Fish-as-Weathervane

Fine Arts Work Center, Provincetown, MA

You were meant for a different blue,
you cod, mackerel, trout, or just idea
of fish, hoisted up, spiked through
the center to test, of all things, air.

Beached in sky, sun beaten, tarnished,
a shred of cloud caught in your gasping
mouth, your turning an illusion of motion
so close to the one for which you were born.

No schools for you there, in that lonely,
elevated place, only its perpetual piercing—
you alien among birds with your useless gills,
useless fins. Caught, darling. Trophy. Stranded

so close to God, you spin in the place
where prayers rise, where dreams of home
take wind and take hold of you like hooks
yanking you—now this way, now that.

August, Charlottesville

After Derek Walcott

In one corner the first match hisses
and soon a chorus of light

answers. Someone shouts *Now!*
and the bright beast stirs,

begins its booted, many-legged march.
Someone raises an anthem

blood and soil: hungry, how it swells,
feeds, roars. Fists of flame

snarl the air, spit snakes of smoke.
Underfoot, the black earth

shudders—mute, immutable; trees
bend with invisible weight.

Above, the black and weary sky
gathers its army of stars.

Grace: A Lamentation

For the victims of the Charleston Shootings

for Cynthia, for Susie
for Ethel, for Clementa
for Daniel, for Sharonda
for Myra, for Tywanza
for DePayne

We only ever wanted grace:
We wanted the ache in our joints
to let up, we wanted a little extra
in the bank, we wanted to retire,
get married, travel, we wanted
dinner—hot and home-cooked,
we wanted a break from the kids,
we wanted to get home to the kids,
we wanted to make someone listen
for once to our side of an argument.
We wanted to write policy and poems,
cross a stage dressed in our full names.
We wanted to see the great-grands
grow into themselves, make sure
that last grown child finds her way.
We wanted to be where we were,
we wanted to be anywhere else.
We wanted to give the weird white boy
a place to rest his obvious angst.
We wanted him to go on his way
and felt bad about it. We wanted,
after all, to do right like the good
book says—to love the neighbor
and the stranger; to welcome both
greatest and least. We wanted only
the grace of our good, God-given lives.

Heaven?

For Sandra Annette Bland

Where does a black girl go
when her body is emptied
of her? And her wild voice,
where does it sing its story
when the knots of history
make a grave of her throat?
What of her future, blue-
broken, unmade? Her name,
—say it!—Sandra, unhoused;
her dreams and memories
lost to their source. Where
does a black girl's love go
when her heart is snapped
shut like a cell door, the key
out of reach as any justice?
And what gift is lost when
a black girl is made a body,
her light dimmed into shadow,
gone? How many angels weep
when a black girl is torn
into wings?

Questions from the Rock

Platia Galia, Serifos

Who will sing you, wandering one,
island sprite? You have made no gardens,
spun no cloth, made memories—
mere footprints—instead of children. You have
taken the faithless wind as your lover,
called yourself daughter of the indifferent sea;
your childhood has wandered off untended,
taking with it the faces that knew you.
Who will know you now?
Who will remember you to your innocence?
You have gathered no bricks for building;
you have let your tongue slacken,
made no prayers to the gods.
You pack your days with glitter and lie
awake at night evading dreams.
When the sleep comes—as it will—
who will travel the dirt roads shouting your name?
Who will know your proper place
and how to number you among your ancestors?
Who will chant your passing until your spirit is safe
across the stars, drifting one—
and will you rest?

II.

Ode to My Parents

Root & reach, you are
the unlike likenesses
haunting my mirror,
possessing my throat:
shout and song. You are
stalwart twin pillars
holding me up—a girl
made so much of air
you lose sight of her
as she sighs her way
into spaces you dreamed
or never thought to.
You who mattered me
into being. You who scored
ocean into my spirit,
placed all my possibility
into the hands of a God
you cannot see but still
believe worthy of faith.
How you hold me still,
your disappeared daughter,
your prodigal progeny
whose return you celebrate
again & again, whose absence
you read as testimony
not abandonment. Beloved
earth from whom emerged
this reckoning of a woman,
the unfed beast of her
hunger. You who pushed
& planted & pruned.
You who promised more
than you could afford
& delivered. You of the open
hands & doors & hearts.
You who let me take
my new name—*Go*.
You who renamed yourselves
Always. You who remain.

Inventing a Lineage on the Day My Mother's Mother Is Buried

For my mother
2/4/16

Today I am conjuring my mother
a mother. She has long fingers
and thin wrists like my mom does,
a wicked right hand—it's genetic.
When my mother was young,
only a meager armful of howling
and flailing, my mother's mother
would pick her baby girl up,
press her lips against her forehead
to trace hieroglyphs into her infant skin,
so when my mother has me
twenty-eight years later, she does
the same thing, the memory still
etched into her. My mother's mother
would not be perfect, of course,
but she'd be pretty close. There'd be
bright lit birthdays and Christmases;
quiet afternoons teaching my mother
to write, her hand wrapped around
her daughter's, curling the letters
of her name. When my mother says
like this, and shows me her perfect
cursive flourish three decades later,
she can say *your granny taught me*
how to write my name like this, too.
My mother's mother will have flaws,
of course: her rice is too sappy;
she makes my mother drink bush
tea when she doesn't want to;
she picks fights when she's tired.
She isn't very good at budgeting,
and is too house-proud for her own
good. Whenever my mother visits
my house in a country far from hers
she'd say *you are just like your grandmother.*

I'd groan and roll my eyes and know
exactly what that means. I wouldn't mind.
When my mother's mother dies,
this imagined version of her, anyway,
it isn't a Monday like any other
with school and bills; I don't forget
it happened; my mother isn't wondering
if now that she's really an orphan
she'll feel more or less abandoned.
The mother I write my mother is worthy
of mourning; when her heart stills,
the grief cuts generations deep—
we'd feel something severed from us
—call it memory, call it love. I would
fly to my mother's side, whisper *I love you*,
my lips pressed against her brow.
My mother is gone, my mother would say,
and a whole, real history would unfurl
to comfort her. I'd close my fingers
around hers and hold on, and by God,
we'd feel something.

I Am Instructed

Wait for the right man,
the right moment,
the right dress. If you're lucky,
the right shoe
might lead you to both.
If not, the right wish—
one without consequences
that disfavor your future
happiness. Wait
for love to descend
like snowflakes,
only less wet, less fleeting.
Wait to be spoken to.
To be seen and attended.
To be taken, seeded,
to ripen and burst.
To be suckled, tugged
into the mothering
dress of watch and worry.
Wait for the thickening,
for youth to fall from you
like a cloak. Wait for gray
hair, fine lines, and the new
music your joints make
in the morning. Wait
for the inevitable wandering
eye to unhook from you
(too dull now to catch it
or keep it). Wait
for the kids to finish school,
to finish college, wait
for him to come back
to his senses. If he doesn't
wait anyway: to act
would be rash; to act
would be unwise. Wait

for the storm to settle,
wait to talk to someone—
a therapist, a BFF, a good
divorce lawyer, even.
Wait before wading
into the deep pool of regret.

When Daughters Drown Their Fathers

After Patricia Smith and Tiana Clark

You cannot ask a pond to be an ocean,
an anthill to be a mountain, or rather

you can, but you will be disappointed
—resent the pond's visible shoreline,

crush the un-awesomeness of the anthill
beneath your tantruming feet. You cannot

ask a man to be more than the sum
of his history and desires, more than

his silences filled with a dead father
& six siblings & the breakback work

that crushed all dreams of high school
or dreaming. You, daughter, want skyscrapers

& degrees & nothing his hands understand
& hate him when he offers in his slow, black

drawl the song of *why* and *wait*. You
purge him like a poison, cut your eyes

at his face in yours—you, daddy-in-drag,
wearing his small-toothed smile, his dark face.

You stomp *no* on any anchor, refuse
any limit but the horizon, rename yourself

endless, and him, *outgrown*; you bury him
with the bright blue mists of your future,

set sail and never look back.

On the Bridge of a Border between Two Countries—

Imagine, if you will, the checkpoint. The guards
in their khakis and hats, their dull plastic buttons.

Imagine the traveller, perhaps it is you in the other life
you always imagined—a grungy backpack and long hair—

nothing but an itch to drag your boots on someone else's
dust. Shake it all off—no shitty job, whiny kids, no nagging

girlfriend hinting about diamonds and commitment,
no envelopes with their hungry windows grinning your name.

When the guard beckons, you show him your crisp blue
passport. He calls you *Sir*, and stamps it without a thought.

Freedom is a bridge, solid beneath your feet; it is the new
country opening to you like a blank check. You grab it. You run.

*

Imagine the other side: the throngs lined up since dawn—
the women shushing kids who fidget in their best shirts;

the men with earnest eyes. Let's make you one of them,
just for fun. You have a letter from a cousin saying *Come!*

and your whole savings strapped to your stomach like a skin;
You *have nothing to declare*, you tell the man scrutinizing

your face, overlaying the image onto the paper he holds
up close to his face. You notice his veined white fingers,

so different than your own–stumpy and spider-brown.
You clutch the bright cloth bag holding all the reasons

you are here, but small enough for the week-long trip
the letter says you are taking. Your wife and children

smile, unblinking in the polaroid zipped into a pocket
you hope won't be searched, lest you betray your grief.

You kissed them, each one this morning, promised to write.
But first this. Answer the guard's questions steadily,

as though nothing is at stake: where you're headed
when you cross that bridge. When you plan on coming back.

Visa Villanelle

First, the gathering of proof, your life's story
reduced to a paper jam of required documents,
evidence of the right shape of your history.

Surrender every expectation of privacy:
release the statements, provide your fingerprints,
prove you have nothing to hide. Your life's story—

unremarkable in its mundane trajectory
of dream, desire, struggle, overcoming—testament
to the harmless shape of your history.

Leave home at midnight. Drive through the wee
hours to arrive at the embassy door first
with your gathered proof, your rehearsed story.

Stand in the chilled, street-lit dark. Pray the rosary.
Repeat again and again to still your heavy-beating heart:
You have evidence, all the right forms; this is but a footnote in your history.

Dawn. Sunlight opens the day like a key.
Wipe the weary from your eyes; enter. State your intent.
Offer the proof of your life: tell its story,
provide evidence. Give it the shape that will become your history.

Gretel of the Caribbean

She loves the forest   all dark
& leavespeak   an ocean
of roots with winged fish
peckish & beaked. She is
a wild thing there, ribs
& hair   a gloaming of a body.
& what was mother here
but the cool velvet of moss,
father, the applause of pebbles
underfoot.   No *lost*. Only direction-
   less drift, only *here*. (I
have been speaking to you
in the tongue you best understand)
& what is witch here
but another name for season,
a necessary turning. Home,
the blue shore   the inescapable
   sweetness of sky.

Return

After Dionne Brand

As if you'd ever truly left.
Even with the betrayal of your tongue
shedding its accent like a snake
sliding out whole from its old skin.
Even with the way you took
to backra's ways like a duck to water.
Even if you became Black,
cloaking yourself in another history.
Even if you say home now
and mean both there and here,
like any cheating bastard who
can't decide which woman's heart
to break, and so shatters them both.
As if you don't look back, unveil
your secret heart and know
no allegiance lives there to anything
but the twins of memory and possibility.

Self-Portrait on the Anniversary of His Death

For Anton

There's a woman at a desk
in a strange country. It is evening.
She types without looking at the keys,
but stares instead out of her window
where invisible birds are rioting
with song. *The nerve of this day,*
she thinks, angry at the spring
light, the bright green trees
sequined with buds, the wind
actually *wafting* through it all,
as though this were a production
of paradise. She knows better:
if there could be heaven on earth
he would be here.

She Who Wears Horns and Weeps

(a lament in two voices)

1.   Hera

They call him thunder, but he falls
like rain at the sight of any female
flesh—any rouged lip, curve of hip,
any flash of nipple, pink of tongue.
I would incinerate his immortal cock,
harvest his balls like ripe figs,
but my eternity is bound to his
by the fat lashes of heat and heart:
I am cursed to love the thirst of him.

2.   Io

For love of me, he held me
face down in the grass. He summoned
a cloud to pillow my head
as he pushed himself between my legs.
I said I was a virgin, sworn
to serve his jealous wife, Hera, and he
came, a burst of god seed.
For my safety, he changed me again,
made a new beast of me.

3.   Hera

If they are his meat, I will carve
them to bone and shadow
before him. If they are water,
I will dam them, poison their wells.
If they are the pleasure of his eyes
I will monster them. What is luminous
I will gutter; what is peaceful
I will ache, as I ache: to madness.

4.　　Io

A gadfly, Hera? Buzz and bother?
I can no longer walk upright.
I have no arms to hide my shame.
I lost laughter and human tears;
I grieve in a foreign skin. I cannot wash
his slick from my body, his grunts and moans
as he fucked me, wild with his lone passion—;
wings and sting to punish me, Hera? As if.

Madame X—

she a hustler a hussy shaking her bustled booty
up and down town all smiles and wiles and whiffs
of possible // naughty naughty now you see her
whipping her hair waist corseted in shiny leather
now you see her buttoned to the throat flashing
a rogue ankle a sweet-boned wrist // now you see
her veiled all eyes and imagination and longing
heart strumming a set-me-free song just for you
for you // for you // maybe she will open her
mind her mouth her sweet-meat sumptin' sumptin'
maybe she'll let you touch-kiss-take everything
you can wrap your words around // starting here //
starting with her goddamn name

Nostalgia Negra

How easily it happens, the slide
into your adolescent self: at a party
the music romps through the air
and you're standing there, drinking
a beer, the beat unwinding you.
The first boy (no, these are men)
comes by, sweeps the pretty blonde
onto the floor; next the willowy
hippie with her sideways smile.
The other girl refuses the two men
who try to pull her onto the floor—
I don't like bachata, she says, flits away.
You swallow more beer, and the words
I do! They go away, disappointed.
For hours and beers, you smile
and small talk with your friend
who buys you another beer,
and then takes the pretty blonde
out for a spin. Everyone melts
into the music and each other,
a tangle of arms, sweeps of legs,
and face it, you know your abandon
—sweaty, unmuscled, thick and black—
has no legible beauty. It jiggles.
It is the opposite of lithe. It lacks
grace. The dance is light and swirl
and lift and everything you are
is too wide, too heavy to be held.
You have learned this lesson before.
You're still learning not to care.

Self-Portrait with Neo-Nazi Demonstration

Leipzig, Germany 4/20/15

Just like that the day is black
and blue, bruised with hate.
Just like that my skin, black
as fine leather stretches so tight
I might tear into bright black
ribbons. See the flag—spent
and flaccid—the windless black,
red and gold clutched in a fist
that I fear will name my black
face dirt, and land. And so, just
like that plans fade to black—
a sunlit walk home folds flat
into a taxi's steel skin, the black
seat holding my body upright.
See the street draped in black
uniforms, the shrill blue shout
of sirens, the march of black-
draped demonstrators, faces set
toward the sun in rows of black
sunglasses. I want to shoot
something, to become a black
grizzly and claw someone's throat:
what I mean is I want to be black
and brave, but today, I am not.
Just like that.

Horror, Too, Has a Heartbeat

They are students and pastors, doctors and teachers. They walk their dogs in parks, and plant perennials under backyard trees. They are runners, readers, car-lovers, coffee-drinkers; they know how to pick a bottle of wine and the best cuts of meat. They say good morning, ask about our days, talk about the weather. They slink past us, invisible and unnamed. They hold the doors for us, give directions to strangers passing through town. With their broad or slender hands they touch us.

They call home the same cosmic nation of which we are all citizens; they, too, are émigrés to the countries of flesh. They are our neighbors. They are our kin. At night, they close their eyes and descend into the old country, confuse its formlessness for shadows. Sometimes, they turn their backs and walk so deep into the mist all the pathways disappear; when they open their eyes they are no place they recognize. They wander the landscapes of mismatched realities, carrying their given or earned burdens. Sometimes the carrying kills them. Sometimes it kills us.

Love is like a language their tongues have forgotten how to move in. It lies in them, a trapped and withering worm. Sometimes they pluck it out, crush its squirming under their boots. Sometimes its writhing drives them closer to some unspeakable edge as they watch us live inside our ordinariness, wear it like skin. They press against the borders of us, ticking with despair or bitterness or hate. They want in. They want us to come out. With desperate and hungry hands, they reach for us.

The Manager's Tips for Working at the San Francisco Restaurant and Bar

New York, NY

He said to my breasts: you're hired.
He said: you're going to be in training for six weeks
and I don't pay trainees. You work for tips.
He said: I'd show off my assets more
if I were you. He said, I'd turn on that million-dollar smile
no matter what kind of day you're having.
He said, men drink more if they think you're really listening
to them: lean in. Especially in the right dress. He said,
go on, Hector wants to dance with you. He said,
loosen up. He said, nobody likes a stuck up bartender.
He said, if anyone asks, it's always best to be nineteen.
He said, if someone wants to buy you a drink, let them.
He said, watch Ruthie work, she knows the ropes—
look at her swing. (Her red hair crawls with a drunk man's fingers.)
He said: Honey, I'll give you a tip for free;
how this goes is entirely up to you.

After 18 Years, the Immigrant Goes to Therapy

Too much loss, too much movement,
too many memories sewn shut
and splitting at the seams, too many
pounds gained, lost, gained
again, too much distance from God,
your mother, your childhood,
too much guilt, too many people
you love too far away, too much leaving
behind, too much not looking
back, too many hopes pinned to you,
too much skin in the game,
too many games—the stakes: too high,
the terror: too constant,
the need: too intense, too ignored,
too expensive—too much
staying strong, dusting off, starting over,
too many jobs, too many bills,
too much homework, too much ambition,
too much being good, being great,
being the best, being worthy,
too much burden of proof, too much,
too much, too much.

Variations in Blue

For Frank X Walker

FXW: *I don't know how to swim*
Me: *What?!*
FXW: *There were no pools for Black Folk when I was coming up*

In sleep's 3-D theatre: home,
a green island surrounded
by the blue of ocean. Zoom
to the heart, see the Couva
swimming pool filled with us
—black children shrieking
our joy in a haze of sun; our life-
guard, Rodney, his skin flawless
and gleaming—black as fresh oil
—his strut along the pool's edge,
his swoonworthy smile; Daddy
a beach-ball-bellied Poseidon,
droplets diamonding his afro;
my brother, hollering as he jumps
into his bright blue fear, his return
to air gasping and triumphant.
And there, the girl I was: dumpling
thick and sun-brown, stripped
down to the red two-piece suit
my mother had made by hand,
afloat in the blue bed of water,
the blue sky beaming above.
When I wake up, I'm in America
where Dorothy Dandridge
once emptied a pool with her pinkie,
and in Texas a black girl's body
draped in its hopeful, tasseled bikini,
struck earth instead of water,
a policeman's blue-clad knees
pinning her back, her indigo wail

a siren. I want this to be a dream,
but I am awake and in this place
where the only blue named home
is a song and we are meant to sink,
to sputter, to drown.

Dis/location

After Southworth's Introduction to Modern Microscopy (*1975*)

You are
split into two parts:
as in before
and after;
the camera itself
and what lives
on the other side
caught
in a plate-glass gaze.
You walk through
so many chambers
to find yourself—
detected.
By which you mean
your name is *specimen*.
By which you mean
your name is *seen
only under scrutiny.* You
deflect by any means
observable. The resolution
is sufficiently enhanced
for the gaze to reach you
even this far down
the spectrometer.
Look. You're crystal
clear and fragile
as a bulb, by which
you mean sometimes
you're only a projection—
your own best trick
of light.

Self-Portrait with Burning Crosses

Dubuque, IA. April, 2016.

There isn't enough water
to make a mirror,
enough light to give back
the faces wearing night
like armor. I've got
nothing to hold on to
in this white ass town
with its white ass worries
where someone decides
to ignite America
into some again-burning
greatness. I'm in the capital
talking poetry and witness
when I read the news
and try to put out the flames
that crawl across my skin,
forget it. But my tongue tastes
like ash. My hands wisp into smoke,
hold nothing but history. Fury
explodes bright and without
mercy: I become the burning.

Who struck the match? Who
pulled out this white hood,
this fiery robe? A student?
That woman in the bank,
with glasses and frosted hair?
The brown-toothed old man
who shuffles down main street
every morning at eight?
Was it the surly couple
across the street or the one
who smiles wide and distant
at once? Was it a lone wolf
or a gang of pimpled teenage boys
regurgitating the diet of Fox news
and hate they'd been fed their whole lives?

I'm a woman with skin
that summons crosses and flame.
Which is to say I am always burning.
Which is to say I do not have enough
tears to put myself out.

Prodigal

Home is the place where, when you have to go there,
They have to take you in.
—Robert Frost, "The Death of the Hired Man"

I lay my body, corpse-like, under the sun,
pull my mother's love over myself like a blanket.

She brings me steaming bowls of broth,
the heads of fishes bobbing inside them;

she strokes my back, her hands seeking
to soothe the wounds neither of us can see,

but ache us both. She asks no questions,
leaves me alone after a time & I give

my tears to a pillow, to the dark earth
of my wanderer's regret. Later, I find her

in the garden, wrist deep in dirt. She
tells me, *Each root is a tear I have not shed.*

I am no good at growing things.
I stare at the sky, night spilling its ink

across the evening. I try to read the stars,
but I have forgotten the language of light.

She says nothing, and I answer with silence.
What is there to say when I've broken my own heart?

III.

What the Living Know

We disappoint.
We forget our dreams.
Fear beats inside us like a second heart,
and we dance our days to it.
Our bodies confound us;
in return we hurl them
against the edges of safety—
highways and drive-thrus,
men with dangerous smiles—
or else we make gods of them
(which means the same).
We manacle our spirits
to this world, name it
living.

Arrival

You look at the ocean, its fathomless blue, luminous. You look at the brown mountains rising like fresh bread, swollen with some livingness, ready to be bitten into. You are in Serifos, and you are not in Serifos. The blue of this water, its own, but calling from you so many other waters: Maracas, Bosphorous, the Gulf of Persia, all lapping at the shores of your memory. You have so many mountains inside you; they are your bread, the food of your soul. Serifos is Serifos, and every island that has come before it. Serifos is Serifos and every wave of blue.

How everything belongs to something else, nothing untainted by memory, or the experience of what has preceded it. How it is impossible to be just one thing in this world of so many entrances, so many openings falling one into the other. A hibiscus blooms at the Benaki in Athens, and another answers at the gates of the house your father was building in Trinidad, in a small village surrounded by cane which is disappearing, eaten by cement and new roads. Even the ruins of the untilled land will soon be gone. Your father no longer lives in that house, where the hibiscus has been replaced first by buttercups, then gingerlilies, now topiary of green flowerless shrubs. But Greece calls it and it answers and is here.

How we wait to be called, suddenly, without warning. What has been calling you here? To what are you the answer? Serifos is answering the call of the disappeared in you. Calling the sugar and the waters of home, calling the longing for a place so simple you might remember who you are, the components of your being—the white house with the flat roof in a village so small you might forget it is where you spent your childhood. You remember yourself mostly as someone who left, who has forgotten the air gritted with the ash of cane fires, the house with no door and a leaking roof, but Serifos asks you to remember. Serifos demands with the dirt road that leads to your blue door, with the palm trees that brood in its heat, in the way you lift your face towards its holy sun. Serifos calls you home.

Red Pilgrimage

I wanted the mountain
but found the absence of river.

I wanted stone
but it was the trees that called

and reached their branches
out to my seeking hand.

I wanted red
and the red earth parted

and bade me pass.
I walked until my feet became red

roots, slow as the trees
snarled into the riverbank.

I wanted the mountain
and saw I was at its beginning:

when I touched it,
it crumbled red into my hand.

In my palm, a compass—
red I could hold on to.

I wanted the pinnacle
but found the riverbed, dry

and brimming with so much
open, the ghosts of things showed

themselves—hovels, nests,
half-buried sticks, bits of burning

white quartz, stands of snake
grass long and green, poets

in search of things that have no name
but red. I wanted wisdom,

but was given a journey:
footstep after footstep,

I made my way through
grief's stubborn endlessness

back into body and time.
My life awaited me, glittering.

I moved toward it—my red heart
pulsing its red river, red air

feeding my red lungs, my red breath
returning, returning. Red

blossoms inside me breaking open.

Maypole

With Ensemble Gallelli

You're eight and excited—
your skirt is full and flagrantly flowered,
your shoulders are bare as they never are—
it's the first Sunday in May,
and you will be dancing in a circle of girls
and boys, twisting ribbons into bright doilies.
You've been practicing hard,
and now the music billows gaily into the air,
the beat swinging your nerves into a smile,
one-and-two-and-three-and.
Your body, your engine heart, feel so light
they might take flight if not for the ribbons
holding you fast to yourself.
Remember it? The bright day, your fairy feet
lifting off and landing, the entangled strands
beautiful, painlessly undone.
You are eight, alive and spinning like a world.

Kalimera

The day shimmers before you, a banquet,
stirs your hunger. To swallow
the yellow disc of sun, the whole
rainbow of blue, the white points of sailboats
and houses, the silver veined stones
and purpling thyme, the pink bodies
and the brown bodies slick and glinting
in their beds of sand, the rioting birds
throating their delirious songs,
the cotton hush, the lurking moon,
the steep ascents and slow-climbing cars,
the chickens squawking in the monastery yard,
the soft-eared donkey, mischievous cats,
and half-naked children, the loaded tavern tables,
the honeyed air, the mad eruptions of glee
and the sweet indescribable grace of it—
you rise for this.

Kalinichta

Close your eyes in Serifos and you fall
into the river of sighs. Night slips you
a token for safe passage—a red bud,
a seashell carrying the sound of the sea.
When the vessel arrives, a raft of wishes,
a puffing steamboat heart, an olive branch
braided with white ribbons, do not hesitate
to board. Do not ask where you are going,
or how you will get back to your firm bed
and your soft breathing body, islands away
now. Give your token to the river. Enter.

Taverna Alexandria

The women fist and batter dough into circles.
The men fan coals into a red mountain of light.
A couple shoulders the music between them,
whispers the ground with their feet. The trees, too,
arch deep toward the dust, unbend into the dark.
No one looks for the moon, raising instead glasses
golden with wine. The wind enters in all its languages.

Portrait

The old man and his donkey walk everywhere—
from Lidvaki to Hora, up the steps of the white city
and back, along the Aegean shore. These days, they walk
through the poems of strangers. They are slow
as time; they carry ladders, windmills, and ghosts.
They are silent, the donkey and the man, swirling
amidst all this unfamiliar language. Sometimes, the man
lifts his arm and waves, or turns an untranslatable gaze
to the eyes making an image of him as he passes.
Mostly, he keeps walking, the donkey keeping pace
behind him, the road bending far beyond the lines of sight.

Blue

The instant you plan to put your head into the water, your mother's voice bells in your skull *don't go getting on wild in the water, eh*. They say at 32 you begin to become your mother, and not a week past that birthday her admonition pulls your body back from a juicy plunge into the Aegean's seductive blue. In your childhood she refused permission to any outings involving water; *you think you a fish*, she'd say, *and my heart can't handle bad news*. A woman now, you know the force she feared, the way water can draw you out; how easy it is to go and go, and never miss the earth beneath your feet until you need it; how sometimes, it gives you no way back. You dive in anyway, the way she always has, headfirst and with a whoop of glee. You know, too, what she loved about the sea—how it is impossible to be burdened in it, how it can strip the body down to its purest, most joyful self. She knew the salt kiss cravings in you: *when you have to go, I will take you*. You swim out now, her voice looped around you like a lifesaver. There is nowhere you can go that it will not find you.

Return

The English, noxious and unmusical, clatters
in your head. You cannot find the smell of the sea,
and nothing is the right shade of blue. The night
is full of fireworks, small streaks bursting into wild,
showy displays that make you squirm. See how happy
everyone is that you're home? says your lover,
soft fingers lacing into yours. You squeeze back,
bewildered by this darkness, its strange stars.

Home in the Key of Absence

It's a slow song—
the kind that invites
reach and clasp and stay,
that summons tongues
to bridge the gap between
two harmonic hungers.
Memory croons
blue as a new morning,
stars blanketed in her throat,
remember, remember,
and wherever you are
you obey, captive.
You know all the words—
convent girl, cane fields,
Sunday morning mass,
Mummy's eyes, daddy's hair,
your sister's skinny legs,
your brother's sweat.
The saltwater chorus
of the ocean. You sing
the harmony to her
nostalgic baseline,
close your present eyes
and slip in to a melody
easy and familiar as skin.
Call it home.

Father, Christmas

You brought us the tree—a real one,
packed the pine into a bucket of dirt,
lay newspapers to catch the needles,
turned the tree this way and that
until it bristled, showed its fullest side.
You hummed and kept one eye on
the news as we sang carols and argued
over the perfect placement of candy canes
and lights. You lifted us—too small, then
— to the top of the tree, the silver star
gleaming in our hands. Christmas
morning, you waved us to church,
and we returned to a feast-laden table:
the bread you slow-kneaded; the ham
steaming, pink; *chow chow* laced with heat.
How we devoured your love, hungry
as only children are, we who knew so little
of the price of such sweetness—the full belly,
the brightly wrapped boxes of expectation,
the laughter gurgling over the surface
of next month's bills, the prayers for grace—
we only ever wanted more.

Ode to the Fish-as-Weathervane

Fine Arts Work Center, Provincetown, MA

You were built for a different blue—
for oceans, rivers, clear complexes of glass
—but here you are, hoisted
among the clouds, neighbor to the stars,
your fins redefining wings.
Say flight. Say sky is ocean by another name.
Say biology is one order of being,
but imagination is another.
How you undo cliché with your unlikely
grace, slip through the clumsy nets
limits would knit around your bizarre
existence. *Token*, they whisper, *freak*.
But how you withstand the fickle
transformations of weather, read
the revolution wind scripts onto your body,
learn to move in its midst. Say evolve.
Say the first order of being is survival.
Say these gills will become lungs
and testify. Say thrive in any element
and name it possible.

What Night Knows

After Gaugin's Le Cheval Blanc

Some women ride horses.
Some women are horses.
Some horses are wolves
Who have lost their teeth,
And are ridden by women.
Some wolves are horses
Ridden wild with dreams.
Some women are dreams
In the shape of horses
Free of the ghost of wolves.
Some ghosts are women,
Their bent air a kind of riding.
Some women ride dreams
And bend the air, freeing
The ghosts and the wolves
And the horses.

Honeyfish

The catch is so fresh, each bite is blue—
the sea still in it, and settling on your tongue

like prayer. This is what it means to eat,
you think, to abandon utensils for the grace

of fingers, to hold flesh against flesh,
hands slick with what will become

inseparable from your own thrumming
body. As a child, you loved *fry dry,*

the small fish you ate whole, and imagined
them swimming in you, your belly

full as an ocean. Now you know better—
that nothing consumed lives on as before.

When the bone, thin as a wish,
lodges itself in the pink flesh of your mouth,

refuses offerings of bread or water,
becomes an ache that will not be moved,

you understand: this is what it means
to be a body—that what is taken in

takes root in ways beyond your choosing—
a single bite and you carry the ocean in your throat.

Elegy for the Closing

First, you learn that brick can be
a blooming. That your hands could welcome
the work of weeding and watering a garden.

You discover the music of a door—
the heft of it sighing on its hinges, the *thwack*
as it swings shut certain as a palm held up.

And the wood! Brown rivers carving
the continents of hundred-year-old plaster
into countries you citizen with your hunger

and dreams, shit and shoes, your need
to be both beloved and alone: your heart learns
the living depths of them. The sun teaches you

your failures at the small duties of love—
the dust scripting window sills, their fogged panes;
the scrawl of mildew in the bathroom;

the porch light's missing bulb throbbing
like a sore tooth. The thousand annoyances, too,
you learn how to conquer or embrace:

bless the fireplace always losing its pilot;
bless the boiler's drawl and slow heat;
bless the toilet running like a winter nose;

bless the cracked, frozen garden hose;
the driveway's perpetual demand for a shovel.
Here, you learn how to root, to become

one who stays, despite. The first lesson
you learn of home is how to be held.
The last, how to gracefully let go.

Ode to Ghosts

It is difficult enough to believe
the daily: the solid way a pan sits on a stove,
and water bubbles certainly around
the curve of an egg; the implausibility
of faucets and coffee makers.
And that's just this morning's magic.
How you must miss it, mourn
in your bodiless kingdoms this world
of old boots and tractors, gizmos
to tell you the way from anywhere
to wherever, coffee crumb cake
and brooms. You cannot know even,
what is felt in your passing,
the brief staticking of the real—
a hair at instant attention,
the spine's stiff salute, blood's cool
response to your fretted or aimless drifting.
What reproach you must hurl
at our lumbering and mindless heft,
O, weightless ones, as we long for lightness,
curse our bones and bellies, the stubbornness of flesh.
How you come, whittled to essence
and occasional voice, recalling to us
our first name and power, all that makes us: matter.

Elegy

For Tamir

This was going to be a curse poem—
me hexing the man who ghosted you,
slivering his days into two-second
increments of agony. I began writing
the playground you could make of his body,
surfing his blood, making monkey bars
of his ribs, dancing his heart's rhythm
on his neck—an inexhaustible mischief,
an incorrigible spirit of boy let loose
in the white country of the murderer's
unshielded body. I would wish him dead,
but I want him nowhere near the realm
he exiled you to, so instead I composed
a soundtrack for his nightmares, a mixtape
of your laugh/the gurgle of your blood
exiting the wound he gave you/a festival
of sirens/your sister's scream/bang/repeat.
This, I understand, is the grief talking.
This is the unchained melody of rage.
But to write his haunting is to name you
hell and you have been misnamed enough,
sweet boy. I make of these words an altar,
instead. I breathe this poem into a prayer,
each syllable a taper burning in memory
of you. Sweet boy, let me build you here
a new body, radiantly black, limber, poised
to become its most beautiful becoming.
Let it be spirited with starsong and rich
with tomorrows. Let me make you a life-
time of days honeyed with love: feast.
You are safe here. Let me write you
again into your name, *Tamir*, baptize
you with tongue and tears. *Tamir. Tamir.*
Let me write you a black boy's heaven,
where freedom is a verb conjugated
by your being, where your only synonym
is beloved, blessed, child of the universe.
Instead, I imagine you there, beginning.

A Gathering of Light

For Anton

In your face, dark as midnight.
In the rasp of your voice
scratching against the distance
between us—oceans, cornfields,
years of never enough time.
In the hours we spent on the simple
pleasures—bowls of hot corn soup
from your favorite street vendor,
cold Friday night beer swallowed
under the stars, the crush of bodies
in a *fête* with music so ecstatic
it became our breathing.
In our sturdy drawbridge silences.
In the ocean days. In the restlessness of me,
my aching, endless reaching;
in the unsteady vessel of my dreams,
so slight against the waves that carried them.
In the way you were beacon, compass,
and harbor—marking the place
where home began, anchoring me
to the solid earth of your heart,
safe. In the earth now, your body.
In what must remain. In what must be
given over to memory's safekeeping:
In the way the sky holds you, and shines.

Reading among the Ruins

In the temple's farthest corner
an olive tree stands,

silver-green leaves like a shawl,
its trunk braided

down into the ancient earth:
you are witnessed by it.

A boat hums by, and the fisherman
waves.

An ocean opens within you,
makes your body a shore

upon which memory crashes—
returning, returning.

You feel the walls in you becoming
ruins, holy and broken.

In the sky, a solitary cloud.
You give your words to the wind.

Acknowledgements

Many people and institutions supported me through the writing of these poems, and it is with immense gratitude I attempt to name them all here.

Thank you first to my mentor, role model, and friend, Kwame Dawes, who summoned this book by expecting it of me.

Thank you to my earliest readers of the file formerly known as "Hot Mess of a Second Book": Carolyn Forché, Harry Mattison, Jessica Jacobs, David Mura and Lisa Maria. Thanks to my siren sisters, particularly Samantha Thornhill, and my relay partners Heidi Zull and Danielle Phillips for journeying with me in the making of these poems.

Special thanks to Dr. Joanne Gabbin and Karen Risch Mott, my friends and Furious Flower forever family for their gentleness with me as this "thing" trembled into being. Thank you Nicelle, for your magic. Thank you, Pilar!

To the folks at the University of Leipzig, and the Picador program, especially Sebastian Hermann and Florian Bast; to Cave Canem and Cornelius Eady for the generosity that afforded my first encounter with Greece; To The Writing Workshops in Greece, and the dynamic duo, Christopher Bakken and Allison Wilkins Bakken, for making it possible for me to return and return; to the Fine Arts Work Center and Gabrielle Calvacoressi for the time, encouragement and opportunity; to the University of Dubuque; to the Iowa Arts Council, Creative Capital, and my cohort of fellows; to my comrades at Split This Rock; to New Issues Press and Bill Olsen for saying yes to this manuscript: Thank you.

Thank you to the following journals and anthologies that first gave these poems a home:

A Mighty Stream: "Play" (as "Elegy for Tamir Rice"), "Heaven?"

Academy of American Poets (Poem of the Day): "Variations in Blue"

Colorado Review: "Nostalgia Negra," "Inventing a Lineage on the Day My Mother's Mother Is Buried"

Comstock Review: "Ode to Ghosts"

Crab Orchard Review: "How to Watch Your Son Die," "Killed Boy, Beautiful World," "She Who Wears Horns and Weeps," "Elegy for the Closing"

Folio: "Blue"

Interviewing the Caribbean: "Questions from the Rock"

Los Angeles Review of Books: "Post-Verdict Renga"

Michigan Quarterly Review: "Reading among the Ruins"

Minerva: "Grace: A Lamentation"

MiPoesia: "Hunger, Too, Has a Heartbeat" (published as "Those Among Us")

One: "Poetry Workshop after the Verdict," "Red Pilgrimage," "Father, Christmas"

Poetry International: "Honeyfish"

Porter House Review "Self-Portrait with Burning Crosses," "Self-Portrait with Impending War"

Resisting Arrest: "Poetry Workshop after the Verdict" *The Feminist Wire*: "Madame X—"

Split This Rock Poem of the Week: "Heaven?," "Self-Portrait with Neo-Nazis"

The Grief Diaries: "A Gathering of Light"

The Pierian: "Gretel of the Caribbean," "Prodigal" *Women's Review of Books*: "Ode to Fish-as-Weathervane," "Elegy to Fish-as-Weathervane"

thepoemoftheweek: "What Night Knows"

With thanks to my gone ones—Anton Stewart, Aviane Hunte, Monica Hand—for their imprints on my life.

To my sister, Debra, who is my heart; to my brother, Ray, whose fierce love follows me across oceans; to my Dad who gave more than either of us realizes; to my mother without whom I am not possible: Thank you.

To Catherine Chung, who knows me in all the important ways: Thank you.

To Syb, whose steadfast and joyful presence is an immeasurable gift: Thank you.

As always, I give thanks to God.

Photo by Adriana Hammond

Lauren K. Alleyne is the author of *Difficult Fruit* (Peepal Tree Press, 2014) and *Honeyfish*, (2018 Green Rose Prize, New Issues 2019). Her work has been widely published in journals and anthologies such as *The Atlantic, Ms. Muse, Women's Studies Quarterly, Guernica, The Caribbean Writer*, and *Crab Orchard Review*, among others. Her work has earned several honors and awards, most recently first place in the 2016 Split This Rock Poetry Contest and a 2017 Philip Freund Prize in Creative Writing for excellence in publication. Alleyne was born and raised in Trinidad and Tobago, and is currently Assistant Director of the Furious Flower Poetry Center and an Associate Professor of English at James Madison University.

The Green Rose Prize

2005:   Joan Houlihan
        The Mending Worm

2004:   Hugh Seidman
        Somebody Stand Up and Sing

2003:   Christine Hume
        Alaskaphrenia
        Gretchen Mattox
        Buddha Box

2002:   Christopher Bursk
        Ovid at Fifteen

2001:   Ruth Ellen Kocher
        When the Moon Knows You're Wandering

2000:   Martha Rhodes
        Perfect Disappearance